DEKITI TIRSIA SIRADAS

A Beginner's Manual

Tashi Mark E. Warner

DEKITI TIRSIA SIRADAS

A Beginner's Manual

Tashi Mark E. Warner

wK Books

Dedication

I dedicate this Book to SGM Jerson "Nene" Tortal, whose wisdom and direction have guided Dekiti Tirsia Siradas Kali to become the art it is today. Without his guidance, I would not be writing this book.

Acknowledgments

First and foremost,
I would like to thank *Grandmaster Tortal*,
for all his patience and teachings.

I would like to thank all my students,
for teaching me so much.

I would like to thank *Tim Caves*
(Timmy T, T-Quad the Ginga Ninja),
for being the perfect Uki.

I would like to thank *Nickolas JJ Buckley*
for jumping into my head with a "that's what she said" joke
after every couple of lines that I wrote.

And last but not least, I would like to thank
my partner in crime, *Deborah Mahoney*,
for keeping my feet on the ground,
even when my head was always in the stars.

Table of Contents

Dekiti Tirsia Siradas: A Beginner's Manual

Only the Beginning

Welcome to the wondrous world of Dekiti Tirsia Siradas (DTS) Kali. This martial art, while easily grasped at its basic level, demands years, if not decades, to master fully. The essence of DTS Kali is not only about physical skill but also about mental resilience, teaching you how to protect yourself and your loved ones with whatever you have at hand, be it a knife, stick, axe, or whatever is in arm's reach. Even empty-handed defenses are taught for when the need arises. DTS Kali trains you to be versatile and adaptable.

Personal Growth and Mastery

I have found one of the greatest benefits of training in any martial Artis the personal growth that accompanies the physical training. The journey in Dekiti Tirsia Siradas towards mastery is not just about developing the skills one needs, but also about developing mental fortitude as well.

Like any martial art, consistency is crucial in DTS Kali. I tell my students there are three ways to get good: practice, practice, practice. Regular practice hones your techniques into muscle memory. This discipline extends beyond the training hall, influencing other areas of life and promoting a balanced and focused mindset.

1. The challenges faced during training—whether learning a difficult technique or overcoming a sparring setback—build mental toughness. Practitioners learn to push through obstacles, remain calm under pressure, and approach problems with a strategic mindset.

2. Studying any martial art gives one a deeper appreciation of the culture of the region where the art came from, and training in DTS Kali also offers a deeper appreciation for Filipino culture and heritage. Understanding the historical and cultural context of an art enriches the training experience, fostering a sense of connection and respect for the traditions they represent.

SECTION ONE

What is Dekiti Tirsia Siradas Kali?

Dekiti – meaning to close in, get very close to your opponent
Tersia – meaning close-quarter fighting
Siradas – meaning to penetrate in at any angle

Dekiti Tirsia Siradas Kali is the art that I train. All the indigenous Filipino arts have much merit, each of the grandmasters is deserved much respect. But, much like great chefs, each master will inherently add their own flavor to the art.

The name of the system consists of three words from the Ilonggo dialect. *Dekiti* translated into the Tagalog dialect is "Malapit" or "Dekit". In English, it means "very close or near." Its emphasis is on close-quarter combat. *Tirsia* means "gua sa wala" or "sa tuo" or "quartering in fighting." *Siradas* means "to push the enemy to a corner or an area with a three-corner side," preventing him from escaping or running away from you delivering multiple deadly blows and thrusts. Siradas means to stop your opponent from getting in or out, for the opponent not to be able to penetrate in any angle of attack.

The Dekiti Tirsia Siradas System is part of the ancient Filipino combat and survival systems indigenous to the island of Negros in the Visayan Region of the Philippines. This fighting art is very combative with emphasis on impact and bladed weapons as well as empty hand techniques and even firearms.

Established in 1850 by Norberto Tortal from all his knowledge and exposure to the arts of Negro, it has been handed down from generation to generation. Norberto's son Segundito Tortal was next in line, with his father imparting all the knowledge he had amassed. Segundito then taught it to his three sons Conrado, Balbino, and Francisco. Balbino then began the education of his young son Jerson (Nene) Tortal.

Further development was created from the combined expertise of the Tortal brothers, Conrado, Balbino, and Francisco. Nene Tortal's uncle, Conrado Tortal, was assigned as Chief of Police of Victorias, Negros Occidental, Philippines during the Commonwealth Period. Victorias was a sugar plantation town and there were very frequent skirmishes among the *sacadas* (sugarcane workers). Using their *espading* (a straight, very sharp, medium-length, flat, and thin blade used to cut sugarcane), they would attack rival sacadas and even the police. Being in charge of peacekeeping, Conrado Tortal frequently relied on his Kali to protect the lives of others.

There is one story of a challenge match that Coronado was involved in. Don Gregorio Araneta from Bago City, Negros Occidental invited the famous, number one *bastonero* from nearby Panay Island, Tansiong Padilla of Iloilo to a match against Conrado Tortal, elder brother of Balbino Tortal. The match was to be held publicly during the fiesta of Bago City. The rule was to have both fighters stand on coconut shells and their weapons (stick and dagger) covered with charcoal dust. Anyone marked or stained with charcoal on their shirt will lose. But Conrado was an expert in close-quarter knife fighting. He threw an unconventional *daga* or dagger method of attack that shocked his opponent. Padilla froze for a split second, giving Conrado a chance to successfully penetrate the opponent's defense, causing Padilla to lose the match.

Balbino Tortal, younger brother of Conrado Tortal and father of Grand Tuhon Jerson Tortal Sr, was a member of the National Volunteer Citizens Army. Before the dark clouds of World War II loomed over the Far East, Philippine Commonwealth President Manuel L. Quezon, proclaimed the National Volunteer Citizens Army as a response to the growing threat of invasion by the Japanese Imperial Army. Grandmaster Jerson Tortal Sr. was born on June 13, 1937. Fondly called "Nene" (Nene was the common nickname for a little girl in the Philippines) because of his small stature, "Nene" Tortal was determined to become one of the legendary grandmasters of Kali. Nene started his training early at the tender age of seven with his father Balbino Tortal and later with his Uncles Conrado and Francisco. Even as a child, Jerson Tortal Sr. fought courageously for his country.

During World War II, he accompanied his father, Balbino Tortal, a guerrilla fighter to the many meetings of the Crusader Army, an underground resistance movement against the Japanese Imperial Army on Negros Island. Being a small child, the Japanese did not suspect Jerson performed intelligence for the Crusader Army. He played near the Japanese garrison and befriended them by exchanging wild tomatoes for sugar, all the while gathering information for the underground resistance. "Nene" Tortal stood by his father to the last minute as they fought the Japanese.

One very significant event took place at the closing of World War II. When Balbino Tortal and his family moved to the town of Talisay, Negros Occidental, they encountered a group of Japanese soldiers. The family stopped, then the soldiers took Balbino away. But his son Jerson Sr. still accompanied him.

The Japanese officer ordered Balbino to be killed. A soldier thrust his bayonet, but Balbino sidestepped and evaded it. The officer drew his katana (Samurai Sword) and attacked, but Balbino disarmed him and used the katana to attack him and the rest of the soldiers, killing many of them.

Unfortunately during the fight, Balbino Tortal was trapped among coconut trunks and then shot. Jerson was also attacked but fortunately slid down a deep ravine where the soldiers could not find him. The rest of the family escaped to safety because of the heroism of Balbino Tortal.

Since the early days, SGM Nene Tortal has spread Dekiti Tirsia Siradas throughout the Philippines and throughout the world. In 1958, he was one of the founding fathers of the Negros Bastoneros, as well as many other organizations on his home island of Negros. He also organized full-contact stick fighting events throughout the island. He was a fierce competitor, winning the first Grandmaster Championship in Cebu. SGM Tortal has taught internationally as well as having students in Europe and North and South America. Dekiti

Tirsia Siradas is a strong family system that will last many millennia.

This is where I come in …

My tremendous journey started in 2007. I had been training some Kali with Mike Williams (always working on increasing my martial arts knowledge) when he mentioned that one of his grandmasters was coming to the United States. He asked if I would like to host a seminar at my school. Now, those of you who know me know I love to train in all styles of martial arts, so to me, this seemed like a great opportunity. Little did I know how great of an opportunity it would be. A date was set, and I informed all my martial arts students and friends about this historic event.

The day arrived and Grandmaster Tuhan Nene was at my school. At 5'2" and around 125 lbs., he would not appear as an imposing person … until you felt his essence. Then it was like being in the presence of a predator waiting to pounce on its prey. Totally relaxed but ready for anything. The ease and grace with which he moved betrayed his 70+ years of age. With a grip of steel, he would manhandle young men in their 20s. On that day he taught me his original 12 strikes with the baston as well as a few disarms, and I was hooked. The essence of the style deeply intrigued and completely enthralled me.

A few years later I had the opportunity to go to the Philippines and train directly with Grandmaster Nene. I slept off and on during the 22-hour flight over, catching up on reading and watching the latest movies (not too many martial arts ones). After an uneventful layover in Manila, we took the final leg to Negros, landing at the Bacolod Airport where we were warmly greeted by Grandmaster Nene. All showing proper respect, we boarded an open-air bus, and we were off on the adventure of a lifetime. Leaving behind the more modernized city of Talisa, we headed off into the mountains and jungles of this island nation (I made it sound ominous for mental imagery – cool, huh?).

The trip by bus took about 2 hours up into the mountains, past sugar cane fields and bamboo houses, down dirt roads, and finally across the metal bridge to our destination, Buanos Aries Resort, a hostel for the locals in the mountains. During WW2, the resort was actually one of the local headquarters of the occupying Japanese forces. After the war, it was turned into a more pleasant spot. There were two pools available, fed by the spring water off the mountain. It was very refreshing. There were little shops to buy water and snacks. There was also a local "Starbucks," a small coffee shop where you could get a fresh cup every morning and drink it in a little seated area that served as our breakfast area. Breakfast consisted of fresh mangos, sweet sticky rice, and rolls.

We would normally spend two hours training in the morning and two hours late afternoon, to avoid the heat. The first round of training was heavily focused on footwork, striking patterns, angles of attack, and disarms with the major weapons of Dekiti Tirsia Siradas Kali. SGM Nene is a stickler for details and would make sure everyone was as close to perfect as possible. Line drills utilizing the 12 strikes with an array of weapons along with different ranges and disarms made a great start to a great day. For the second session, we would warm up, run the basics, and then explore a wider range of information from some of the more esoteric weapons, such as the karambit and Wasik (hand axe). I like to say training Kali is like peeling the layers off an onion, and in the second session, we would peel off a lot of layers.

The in-between time is when we would go sightseeing. The transportation we were using at the time was either a motorcycle or a buggy attached to a motorcycle. Usually, I was in the buggy hanging out the side filming with my camera. On one of our first adventures, we traveled up into the mountains to see two beautiful places. The first was a mountain view of the area we were in. Sugar cane fields dotted the countryside, and you could see many of the villages. The second part was a jungle-falls setting that looked like something right out of a movie. The water cascaded down hundreds of feet to disappear at the bottom of a deep ravine.

On another day after the first session, we took a trip to one of the nearby villages where we had a chance to meet and mingle and we were entertained by a group of children practicing their dancing skills. In this village, we were also able to visit the stable of fighting roosters (game cocks). Winners are treated like kings, losers are dinner.

One of the delicacies I had the pleasure of trying was balut. Balut is a fertilized duck egg about 21 days into the cycle, which is boiled and served so it is a half-developed duck. Much of the time in between sessions was spent by the pool, in our cabin/room, or on the patio overlooking the resort.

On the last morning before the flight out, we went to Grandmaster Tortal's daughter Mimi's house outside Talisa. This is a more Western-style house than we are used to in the States. There we had a delicious brunch of food we were used to, and some we were not. We were also treated to a short demonstration of Dekiti knife defense drills by Mimi's two sons and Grandmaster Tortal. Then, all too soon, it was time to get to the airport and be homeward-bound. I've been back to Negros several times since, each time more fascinating than the last. I hope to make it a yearly trip.

Reflecting on my journey since 2007, I am reminded of the many lessons learned and the milestones achieved. Each phase of training brought new challenges and opportunities for growth. The initial stages were about building a strong foundation — mastering the basic strikes, blocks, and footwork. As I progressed, the training became more nuanced, focusing on advanced techniques and weapon applications.

One of the most significant turning points in my journey was the realization of the art's depth. The more I trained, the more I discovered the intricate layers of DTS Kali. It was not just about physical prowess but also strategy, timing, and psychological acumen. This realization motivated me to delve deeper, seeking to understand not only the how but also the why behind each technique.

Teaching others has been another rewarding aspect of my journey. Sharing the knowledge and seeing the growth in my students has been fulfilling. It reinforced the idea that martial arts are not just about self-improvement but also about contributing to the community and passing on tradition.

If you get the chance to travel to Negros someday, you must try the mangos. You will never taste the freshness that you will find there. The same can be said of the art. You'll never get the full sweetness anywhere like you will at the source.

SECTION TWO

The Baston (Stick)

The *Baston* is the DTS weapon that is typically trained first. The baston should be 28 inches in length and 1.25 inches in diameter.

The baston is divided into three sections.

1. The *Punyo*, or butt,

2. The *Shaft*, or middle, and

3. The *Tip*, or head.

Punyo

Comprised of "one handgrip below the gripping hand," the Punyo is used for striking close range, grabbing, locking, and/or disarming.

Shaft

The shaft is primarily used for striking in a hammer fashion in the middle-to-close range, but may also be used for grabbing, chokes, and locks as well.

Tip

The tip of the stick is primarily used for striking, stabbing (Bunyos in the Ilonggo dialect), or thrusting and slashing.

SECTION THREE

Salutation

We will do the salutation at the beginning of each training session to show respect to the art, the culture, and the instructor.

From the starting position, drop the right knee to the floor, raise the right wrist to the center of the forehead (third eye), and the back of the left hand should touch the floor.

Recite, "I seek for knowledge."

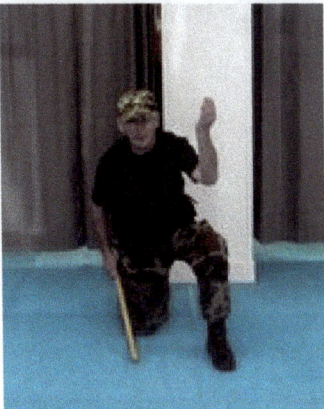

Drop the tip of the baston to the floor and raise the left palm towards the sky, fingertips stopping nose high.

Recite, "I give my respect to the art."

Stand to attention position, touch the Punyo to the center of the chest holding the baston slanted up at a 45-degree angle.

Recite, "I give my loyalty to my instructor."

Drop the left foot back and assume a fighting position with knees bent 135 degrees. The left hand is open in center guard, baston held at a 45-degree angle to the front.

Recite, "I am ready."

Section Four

The 12 Strikes

The strikes are to general target areas, and the type of strike - Hammer, Punyo, Bunyos - will guide the exact target location. Hammer strike is done with the shaft of the baton, Bunyos would be done with the tip of the baton, and Punyo is done with the butt of the baton.

#1 - Left ear diagonal downward

You are striking with a diagonal angle from your right shoulder to the left ear of your opponent.

#2 - Right ear diagonal downward

You are striking with a diagonal angle from your left shoulder to your opponent's right shoulder.

#3 - Reverse diagonal upward

Reverse diagonal upward from the right hip, hitting the opponent's left knee cutting the body and direct to the opponent's lower left jaw.

#4 - Vertical reverse diagonal upward

Reverse diagonal upward from the left hip, hitting the opponent's right knee cutting the body and direct to the opponent's lower right jaw.

#5 - Center thrust to the groin or solar plexus

Center thrust (Bunyos) to the groin up the centerline to the solar plexus. The target area can be anywhere from the groin up the centerline to the solar plexus.

#6 - Lateral strike cutting the left arm floating ribs

Lateral strike from the right shoulder striking the left floating ribs of the opponent.

#7 - Vertical reverse lateral strike cutting the right arm floating ribs

Reverse lateral strike from the left shoulder, striking the right floating ribs of the opponent.

#8 - Center downward strike, hitting the crown of the head

Center downward strike off the right side of the body, hitting the crown of the head.

#9 - Upward circular thrust, hitting the left body and directly to the lower left jaw

Upward circular thrust, Bunyos, hitting the left body and directly to the neck and lower left jaw.

#10 - Upward vertical reverse circular thrust, hitting the right body and directly to the lower right jaw

Upward vertical reverse circular thrust, hitting the right body and directly to the neck and lower right jaw.

#11 - Vertical reverse downward strike, hitting the crown of the head

Reverse downward hammer strike from the left side of the body hitting the crown of the head.

#12 - Center double-hand thrust to the bridge of the nose

Double hand thrust to the bridge of the nose followed by hammer strike to the crown of the head.

Section Five

Footwork

In Dekiti Siradas Kali, footwork is the key, meaning that footwork, body mechanics, and structure of the body make the style of Kali easily adaptable by anyone, regardless of size.

In DTS Kali there are two main types of footwork, although within this footwork you will find all the angles used in Filipino Martial Arts as well as many other arts.

The first footwork series we will cover will be the Advancing Footwork.

Advancing Footwork

This can be done properly with either foot forward. To make it easy to explain our drill, we will start with the right foot forward.

We will first step forward with the left foot, following up with the right. Our left foot is now forward.

Reversing the process, we step forward with the right foot following up with the left foot.

You should practice this footwork forward and backward several times.

The second set of footwork is the defensive footwork. Looking at the diagram above, you can see the many angles that DTS incorporates in its footwork.

We will start with the left leg forward.

From here, step forward with the right leg, and then step behind at a 45-degree angle with the left leg.

From the opposite starting point (right leg forward), we step forward with the left leg, stepping behind with the right leg at a 45-degree angle behind the left.

To practice this footwork set a timer for 30 seconds to one minute and go from the right to the left using the 45-degree footwork. After you get used to the 45-degree angle, you can increase the arch to 90 degrees.

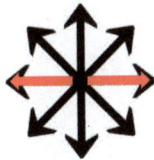

Then 135 degrees.

Then 180 degrees.

SECTION SIX

Hubad Drill

"Drills can be the best of things and drills can be the worst of things."
- Mark E Warner

Performing the Filipino Martial Arts Drill *Hubad* requires not just physical agility, but also mental acuity and a deep understanding of the art form. This drill, rooted in ancient Filipino Martial Arts traditions, serves as a foundational exercise in honing one's reflexes, timing, and sensitivity to an opponent's movements.

The Hubad drill is a very functional drill in teaching the fundamental moves used in reverse countering as well as other needed applications. We must also be able to flow in and out of the drills.

Goals and Benefits

As the drill progresses, practitioners gradually increase the intensity of their movements. The goal is not just to dominate, but also to learn from each exchange, recognizing openings, weaknesses, and opportunities to counter.

Through consistent practice of Hubad, practitioners develop a deep understanding of body mechanics, timing, and distance management—essential skills, not just for self-defense, but also for personal growth and self-discipline. Ultimately, mastering the Hubad drill requires dedication, patience, and a willingness to embrace the dynamic nature of the Filipino Martial Arts.

Hubad Drill

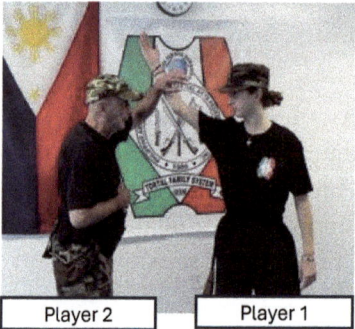

Player 2 | Player 1

To begin the Hubad drill, practitioners stand facing each other, right foot forward. Player #1 initiates a chopping action with their right arm while player #2 will initiate an upward block with the left arm.

Player #2 then uses their right arm to bump up player # 1's right arm.

Player #2 will send player #1's arm over their head re-engaging with the left hand, guiding above the elbow, thumb pointing up, to parry away Player #1's arm.

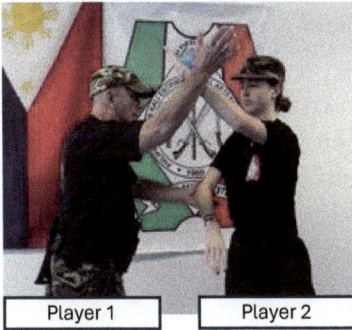

Player 1   Player 2

After this is completed, the roles are reversed, and the drill continues as player #2 initiates the attack. Player #1 chops with the right arm. Player #2 upward blocks with left arm.

Using their right arm, Player #2 bumps up Player #1's right arm.

Player #2 re-engages with the left hand and sends the right arm upward and across to parry the arm away.

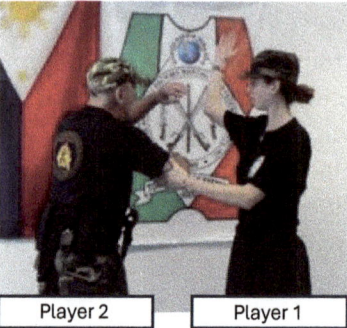

Player #2 now performs the downward chop with their right arm to switch roles and continue the drill.

Player 2 | Player 1

Section Seven

Reverse Countering

Time to put a few things together. Dekiti means "tightly close," and for this disarming series, we want to be tightly close.

Against the #1, #3, or #6 Strike

As the #1 Strike swings in (we start with the left foot to train our footwork), we step with the right foot and out to a 45-degree angle with the left foot. Do a cover block with the left arm, keep bent at a 135-degree angle, strike with the right hand to the body, and shock the body.

From here we will do the Hubad move to get to the outside.

From the outside position slide the left hand down, grabbing the thumb pad and pinky pad, squeezing tightly.

Use the butt end of the stick to pry the opponent's stick out of their grip.

Slide your left hand back up above the elbow so you can control your opponent.

You can retain the opponent's stick and counterattack with two sticks.

Or you can get rid of their stick and counterattack with yours alone.

Against the #2, #4, #5, or #7 Strike

As the #2 Strike is thrown, step to the left with the left foot, stepping back right.

The right hand will strike the opponent's forearm, and the left hand will cup above the elbow, thumb up.

Slide the left hand down to the opponent's hand (palm to palm) squeezing the thumb and pinky.

Disarm with Punyo and rearrange with one stick or retain the opponent's weapon and rearrange with two sticks.

Against #8 Strike and #11 Strike

The #8 and #11 strikes will be dealt with by riding the attack from the outside to a circular snake disarm.

Starting in the on-guard position, use defensive footwork to evade to the left.

Use the baton to guide the arm in a downward fashion.

Diving down, encircle the opponent's arm with your forearm from right to left.

Grasping the opponent's stick with your left hand, push the knuckles of your right hand into the wrist of the opponent to cause a release of the weapon.

You now control your opponent's weapon.

Against #12

The 12 is handled using the 45-degree footwork to the right to stop the strike.

Then, use your stick to go over, under, or through the opponent's arm to set up for the disarm.

From here, use your footwork to get to the other side of your opponent's body and finalize the disarm. Then you may counter-attack.

Against #9 & 10

The defenses against the #9 and #10 strikes are almost identical to all the others. However, these two strikes are stabbing strikes. The way you would want to deal with these strikes would be to use your footwork, then destroy the stick by striking/attacking it. Next, you would proceed with the reverse countering – bumping up and then stripping the #9 strike, and straight to the stripping for the #10 strike.

Against a #9 strike, use defensive footwork to move to the right inside.

Attack the opponent's stick with the shaft of yours.

Grab the arm, …

… then Punyo the body.

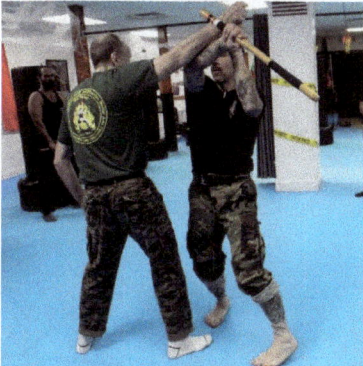

Continue using the Hubad move to get to the outside to finish the disarm.

Against the #10 strike, use defensive footwork to get to the outside.

Attack the opponent's stick with the shaft of yours.

Go directly to the disarm.

Conclusion

Despite the years of training, I am always aware of how much there is still to learn. The path of DTS Kali is one of continuous growth and evolution. Each training session is an opportunity to refine techniques, deepen understanding, and push the boundaries of what is possible.

For those beginning their journey in DTS Kali, my advice is to embrace the process with patience and persistence. The path to mastery is long and demanding, but the rewards are profound. Surround yourself with a supportive community, seek guidance from experienced practitioners, and most importantly, stay committed to your training.

Dekiti Tirsia Siradas Kali has become more than just a martial art; it is a way of life. It teaches practical life skills, fosters personal growth, and instills a deep sense of discipline and resilience. My journey in DTS Kali has helped in my martial arts transformation, shaping not only my physical abilities, but also my character and mindset.

As you embark on your own journey into DTS Kali, remember that the path is as important as the destination. Each step you take, each lesson you learn, contributes to your growth as a martial artist and as an individual. May your journey be as fulfilling and enriching as mine has been. Embrace the challenges, celebrate the milestones, and always strive for excellence.

Join our Tribe

We are always looking for:

- Practitioners
- Instructors
- And future Tuhons (Tribal Leaders)

No matter what style of martial art you practice now, Dekiti Tirsia Siradas Kali will seamlessly flow into whatever you do. It also has stood the test of time as a stand-alone art.

We'd love to help guide you on how to get started in the art of Dekiti Tirsia Siradas Kali. Drop us a line today at tashimark@yahoo.com.

Dekiti Tirsia Siradas Playlist –
Mark Warner's Professional
Martial Arts Academy on
YouTube

Dekiti Tirsia Siradas at Mark
Warner's Professional Martial
Arts Academy Facebook Group

Mark Warner's Professional
Martial Arts/Dekiti Tirsia Siradas
Patreon Content

About the Author

Tashi Mark Warner has trained in martial arts for almost 50 years. In the early 70s, inspired by the likes of Bruce Lee, Tashi Mark started in Kenpo Karate under Richard Ladow. After serving in the US Army, traveling twice to Korea and once to Germany, Tashi Mark found inspiration in the JCVD movie *Bloodsport* and decided to one day open his own school. On April 8th, 1998, his passion project was finally achieved and the doors of Mark Warner's Professional Martial Arts Academy opened. As Tashi Mark likes to say, "If you love what you do, you'll never work a day in your life."

Also in 1998, Tashi Mark started training Northern Mantis Kung Fu and Shaolin Kung Fu with Sifu Scott Jeffery. Since 2007, Tashi Mark has furthered his training, adding Dekiti Tirsia Siradas Kali with Grandmaster Jerson "Nene" Tortal, as well as Baringin Sakti Silat with Grandmaster Edward Lebe.

Tashi Mark is a full-time martial artist.

"One of the greatest things in the martial arts is the transmission of knowledge to the next generation." - Tashi Mark Warner

About the Author

We Want to Hear from You!

Reviews are an important part of how others find our books, and they help us create content you love. If you enjoyed this book, please visit this title's Amazon listing, Goodreads listing, or wherever you purchased your copy, and leave us a review. We will use your feedback to help create more content catered towards you, our loyal readers.

Thank you!!

AVAILABLE FROM WHISTLEKICK BOOKS PUBLISHING

BY JEREMY LESNIAK

Non-Fiction

The Martial Artist's Handbook

12 Months to Health

How Not to Hold a Tournament

Stronger people Are Harder to Kill

Press Release Mastery

Simpler Social Media

Starting to Sell on Amazon

Fiction

Faith: The Katana Chronicles - Book One

The Katana Chronicles - Book Two **COMING SOON!**

BY BARBARA W. MCCOY, MS

It's as Easy as Z to A: A Journey Through the Alphabet

BY TASHI MARK E. WARNER

Dekiti Tersia Siradas: A Beginner's Mannual

BY JENNI SIU

The Origin of Master Hopkick: Beginnings

The Origin of Master Hopkick: Beginnings - Special Edition

The Origin of Master Hopkick: Beginnings - Instructor's Edition (w/ Chris Rickard)

The Origin of Master Hopkick: Lessons

The Origin of Master Hopkick Book Three **COMING SOON!**

BY CHRIS RICKARD

The Instructor's Guide to Jenni Siu's The Origin of Master Hopkick: Beginnings - Mat Chat and Classroom Discussion Guide

BY JENNI NATHER

Modern Moms of Martial Arts: Volume One

BY CHRIS RICKARD AND JENNI NATHER

2-Minute Martial Arts **COMING SOON!**

COMPILED BY FRANK WOOD

The First Cup Joke Book

INSPIRED BY WHISTLEKICK MARTIAL ARTS RADIO

Collections

Celebrating Women in the Martial Arts

Legends of the Martial Arts

What Advice Would You Give Martial Artists 100 Years From Now?

A Journey Into the Badlands w/ Daniel Wu, Emily Beecham, and Sherman Augustus

The Karate Kid & Cobra Kai Collection

Restomp The Interviews w/ Master Ken, Matt Page, and Joseph Conway

One-on-One Interviews

Tony Blauer

Mr. Don "The Dragon" Wilson

Shihan Bas Rutten

Bill "superfoot" Wallace

Adrian Paul

Sensei Fumio Demura

Iain Abernethy

Five Faces of Kempo

Jhoon Rhee

Stephen Hayes

Nathan Porter

Feras Alhlou

⟵ SCAN TO SEE ALL OF OUR TITLES

DON'T MISS OUR EVENTS!

ALL-IN WEEKEND

This 2-day martial arts event will be half training experience and half retreat. The cost of the event includes all of your training, your lodging, food, and an event shirt. All you have to do is show up, and we'll take care of the rest.

FREE TRAINING DAY

whistlekick's Free Training Day is exactly what the name says - one day of the year where martial artists come together to share and learn, all for free. There is no admission fee at this event, instructors are not paid, and whistlekick picks up the tab for the venue and any other logistical costs.

MARTIAL SUMMIT

Martial Summit is our vision for the future. A place where martial artists, from all over the world, of all systems and styles, come together to share. This 4-day event includes Free Training Day Northeast as well as the Never Settle Awards Banquet.

Follow the QR codes above or visit whistlekick.com and click on "For Individuals" to find all the latest info on our incredible events!

12 Months to Health

By Jeremy Lesniak

This book is designed to help you establish and reinforce 12 simple, inexpensive habits to achieve a healthier you in 12 months.

"Mr. Lesniak has laid out a well-researched, simple, and gradual guide to real success in incorporating healthy habits into one's daily life. I look forward to sharing this with my patients as a partner in their journey toward better health."

— Joshua Singer, Licensed Acupuncturist at River Street Wellness, Montpelier, Vermont

"Setting just the right goal is hard to do, and starting with consistent, bite-sized, achievable goals is the way to achieve real change in your health."

— Irvin Eisenberg, Masters in Occupational Therapy, Structural Integrator and Owner of Resilience Occupational Therapy

"Our healthcare system, as it is built, right now, is largely not designed to help you until AFTER chronic disease strikes. Even preventative health endorsed by your doctor is left to the small choices you make daily, by yourself, well outside of the walls of the clinic."

— Joshua T. White, MD, MBA, Chief Medical Officer, Gifford Medical Center

"12 things that ANYONE can do that will make a vast difference to their life."

— Daniel Eagles

"A single focus for a month makes it much more likely that I will be able to make sustainable changes."

— StaciAnne KaeLeigh Grove

FREE whistlekick Flexibility Program!

Yes, I said FREE! This program is designed by and for martial artists with features you won't find in any other program, at any price. The Flexibility Program is rooted in the latest science, immensely effective, and different from what most of us were taught.

The FREE whistlekick 30-Day Challenge

The program is a FREE and COMPLETE standalone training program you can start at any time. It's designed to be done on its own, without other strength or conditioning programs. The daily workouts can be completed in about 10 minutes, require NO EQUIPMENT, and can be done in a small indoor space.

This program combines martial arts and fitness to get you the exact workout you need on that day. It helps you build momentum to gain more out of your time – with your health, fitness, training, and the rest of your life.

These are just a sample of the programs we offer!

Looking to increase your speed? How about your fighting endurance? Visit whistlekick.com to see how we are revolutionizing the way you train to improve not only your martial arts skills, but also your overall health.

Check out the collection of whistlekick Programs in the whistlekick Store today!

SCHOOL OWNERS

wK Alliance

Apply to join

""My school is up 33% since I started working with whistlekick. Whistlekick is the best of the best."

~ Mark Warner

Why join?

Immediate Impact

Elevate your school with expert-led webinars, peer-support, geotargeted ads, and exciting online challenges.

Hassle-Free Marketing

We produce powerful marketing for you, bringing prospective students direct.

Community and Growth

Join an exclusive network of martial arts professionals committed to success and mutual support.

Flexibility and Freedom

No long-term commitments – cancel anytime if it's not the right fit for you.

Expert Guidance

Monthly webinars on vital topics like student enrollment and financial management.

Dynamic Online Challenges

Engage and motivate your students with fun, creative challenges designed with marketing benefits in mind.

We Truly Appreciate You!

Thank you for supporting whistlekick Books. We invite you to visit us at whistlekick.com. While there, you will find links to check out our other books, our store, social media, how to leave us reviews, info on our other projects, and much more.

We are always open to your thoughts, questions, and suggestions. You may contact us anytime at books@whistlekick.com.

Thank you!

wK Books

9 798330 452682